JORDAN REED

Starter's Guide To Real Estate Investment

Explore investment options for beginners and find the right one for you

Copyright © 2024 by Jordan Reed

All rights reserved. No part of this publication may be reproduced, stored or transmitted in any form or by any means, electronic, mechanical, photocopying, recording, scanning, or otherwise without written permission from the publisher. It is illegal to copy this book, post it to a website, or distribute it by any other means without permission.

Jordan Reed asserts the moral right to be identified as the author of this work.

Jordan Reed has no responsibility for the persistence or accuracy of URLs for external or third-party Internet Websites referred to in this publication and does not guarantee that any content on such Websites is, or will remain, accurate or appropriate.

Designations used by companies to distinguish their products are often claimed as trademarks. All brand names and product names used in this book and on its cover are trade names, service marks, trademarks and registered trademarks of their respective owners. The publishers and the book are not associated with any product or vendor mentioned in this book. None of the companies referenced within the book have endorsed the book.

First edition

This book was professionally typeset on Reedsy.
Find out more at reedsy.com

Contents

1. Introduction — 1
2. Why Invest in Real Estate? — 3
3. REIT — 5
4. Syndication — 7
5. Wholesale — 10
6. Long Term Rental — 14
7. Short Term Rental (Vacation Rental) — 17
8. Mid Term Rental — 20
9. Tax Liens — 23
10. Land — 26
11. Lending — 29
12. Conclusion — 32
13. Resources — 33

1

Introduction

Welcome to Starter's Guide To Real Estate Investment! I'm so excited to share the lessons that I learned over the last few years of my real estate investment journey.

I started to learn real estate in 2021. Since then, I have had my fair share of mistakes and lessons learned and I wanted to share what characteristics each investment strategy has so that you make your own decision on what fits you best.

If the investment you're considering is not covered in this book, it's because I don't have first-hand experience. What fall under this category are fix-n-flip, multi-family residential, commercial real estate, section 8, coliving, RV park, mobile home park, and the list goes on.

A brief background about myself... I started my career as an engineer at a tech company and, fortunately, throughout my career, I have been paid well enough to stash some money in my savings account so I started to invest part of it in the stock market. But at the same time, I didn't see my net worth growing at a pace that will support my retirement once

I'm at the age even though I've been trying to maintain my spending at a moderate level. I knew something had to change.

If you are in a similar situation as me, I want to share my notes with you so that you can choose an investment strategy that's right for you faster.

2

Why Invest in Real Estate?

As a refresher, I wanted to go through some points of why investors invest in real estate because I refer to these points in this book.

There are a few reasons an investor buys real estate.

1. Cashflow

When an investor (as a landlord) rents their property to a tenant, the property can produce an income provided that the revenue (the rent) is greater than all the expenses.

2. Appreciation

In many markets, the price of a house goes up (i.e. appreciates). If you buy a property in one of those markets, your money invested in the property may be able to maintain its purchasing power even when inflation causes cash in a bank account to lose its purchasing power.

3. Depreciation

The government wants enough supply of housing for its citizens. In order to ensure that, the government provides those who buy houses (both investors and homestead buyers) with incentives to do so. One of the incentives the government gives to real estate investors is tax depreciation. If their real estate business makes money, the government allows the real estate investor to reduce the taxable income through the depreciation of their real estate assets.

4. Leverage

You can obtain an asset that produces income through borrowed capital. But leverage is a double-edged sword. It can take you down when your revenue gets below your debt service (e.g. mortgage) for whatever reason.

5. Paydown/Amortization

You can pay down your mortgage over a long period of time (typically 30 years). You should structure your deal so that your revenue (e.g. rent) covers the cost (e.g. mortgage payment). In this ideal scenario, your property generates income without ongoing out-of-pocket expenses.

3

REIT

REIT stands for Real Estate Investment Trust that owns, operates, or finances income-producing real estate properties. REITs can be publicly traded, public non-traded, or private. If you are familiar with buying and selling stocks, this is one of the closest forms of real estate investing to investment in stocks.

REITs own (often commercial) properties in various sectors (e.g. multi-family residential, retail, and hospitalities). You buy REIT stocks, mutual funds, or ETFs and your REIT operators manage properties they own. They are required to pay the majority of their income to shareholders as dividends.

This was my first exposure to real estate investing. It was much less intimidating for me to dip my toes into real estate investing compared to getting a mortgage and purchasing a property.

Pros

Accessibility

REIT is a security that trades just like a stock that you might own. You can buy REIT stock, mutual funds, or ETFs through a brokerage firm just like a stock. It's a different asset class, so you need to do your research and due diligence differently from stocks, but the logistics of buying/selling are familiar to many stock investors.

Liquidity

It's highly liquid and easy to buy or sell publicly-traded REITs compared to real estate properties, which could take weeks or months.

Passive Income

While you hold your REITs, you continue receiving dividends without managing properties yourself like you should in some rental strategies.

Cons

Lack of Control

Some investors look into real estate investing partly because they have better control over your investment. With stocks, you won't necessarily hold strong control over how the company in question operates, whereas you get to be involved with the real estate investment as much as you would like. With REIT, it's more like a stock than other real estate investments like rentals. This is the biggest reason I moved from REITs to other more "active" real estate investments over time.

Volatility

REITs and stock markets have different underlying assets so this difference in fundamentals causes them to perform differently than you would expect. While that is true to some extent, they didn't differ as much as I had expected before I started investing in REITs.

4

Syndication

Also known as Crowdfunding, real estate syndication companies provide an alternative way to invest in real estate. These companies pool funds from a group of investors and invest it into an investment property or properties. If you have some money invested in the stock market and you want to diversify, syndication can be a great entry into real estate investing (just like REITs), especially when you have some money to invest in but limited time.

There are two key parties in a real estate syndication, the general partner (GP) and the limited partner (LP). GP is an operator, who finds deals, structures investments, and operates the business. LP is a money guy or gal, who provides capital and stays passive for most of the project.

Some companies provide their members with syndication opportunities such as Fundrise, CrowdStreet, YieldStreet, EquityMultiple, and Realty-Mogul among many others. If you invest through these companies, you will be an LP.

Pros

Passive Income

This is more of a passive play among various strategies discussed in this book. If you started your investment journey with stocks and want to diversify your portfolio, Syndication might be a good entry point into real estate investment, and familiarize yourself with concepts in real estate investment especially if you don't have time to manage properties yourself.

You should do your due diligence on the general partners. What's their track record? How have their past projects been performing?

Use the operator's expertise

If you work with operators who have a long history of successful operations, you can be in a much safer place. It would take many years, even a decade for you to learn the ropes and be able to operate in multi-family residential, retail, and hospitality successfully.

Variety of asset classes

As mentioned before, Syndication operators manage properties in a broad range of fields within real estate. Self-storage or mobile home parks will perform differently from triple net commercial or office space. You can be more diversified this way as opposed to purchasing a single-family home with a mortgage on your own.

Cons

Lack of Control

This is a flip side of the "Passive Income" coin. Being hands-free means you have little say in which deal you want your money to be invested in. For some investors with capital to spare but little time to spend, this is exactly what they are looking for, but if you have a specific preference, you might prefer more "active" avenues of investing.

Illiquid

Once you participate in syndication, you cannot pull your funds at least for 5 or 7 years typically. You should be ok with parting from your money for several years.

5

Wholesale

As a wholesaler, you play a middleman that connects a seller of a property and a buyer. You sign a contract called a Purchase and Sale Agreement (PSA) to buy a property (in many cases at a discount) with a seller. This gives you an "equitable interest" to the property and, as a result, a right to market **the contract** (please note that you're not allowed to market and sell **the property** itself unless you are a real estate agent). As long as the state in question does not have a law (often called a House Bill) prohibiting you from marketing and selling the contract without a real estate agent license, you can sell or find a buyer and "assign" the contract to them for a fee (called an assignment fee). The buyer of the contract completes the transaction with the seller. This is a great way to enter into real estate investing because it requires a relatively low cost of entry.

There are many reasons that a seller sells their property at a discount. They might have a new job offer in a different city, state, or country, so they have to sell and move relatively soon. They might be going through a divorce. An owner might have passed away and the heir does not want to have to do with the property.

WHOLESALE

There are many reasons that a buyer buys a property through a wholesaler. These buyers can be investors whose main income source is their fix-n-flip business. They are busy renovating houses and don't have time to look for houses to renovate. Another type of buyer doesn't have stellar credit scores and is ineligible to get a conventional mortgage from a bank.

There are two sides to the business, acquisition (buying) and disposition (selling). If you do business all by yourself, you will do both acquisition and disposition, finding and talking to both buyers and sellers. If you work on a team, you might do either acquisition or disposition.

Pros

Low barrier of entry

Wholesale requires close-to-zero entry costs. Especially if you work for a team that does wholesale, you don't have to pay for infrastructure such as mailer, dialer, and Customer Relationship Management (CRM) software.

Shorter turnaround

Wholesale transactions are much shorter compared to fix-n-flip for example. If you lost your job and need income quickly, wholesale is best suited among all the other options in this book. Wholesale is about today's money.

Beginner friendly

You get to learn about real estate transactions. You'll also learn how to comp and underwrite a deal. Underwriting is a valuable skill in any type of real estate investment.

Location independence

Many wholesalers do deals across the country. You can buy and sell properties virtually without having to be in the same room with your buyer/seller when signing the contract.

Proven method

This is a proven method to make full-time income. Once you establish your deal flow, it is totally possible to replace your W-2 income with a real estate wholesale business.

Cons

Active Business

Wholesale is an active business. When you stop working on acquisition and disposition, you'll stop earning income from the business (in contrast to most buy-and-hold strategies like Long Term Rental, with which you continue earning income at least for a while without putting in the same amount of work constantly).

Competitive

Since the barrier for entry is so low, it's a somewhat competitive space.

Not able to enjoy tax benefits through depreciation

Wholesalers make profits through transactions and don't necessarily own any properties, so they don't get to enjoy any tax benefits that come from ownership of properties such as depreciation.

Regulation

Some states (Illinois and Virginia are the most prominent ones) started to pass laws to regulate real estate wholesale practices. In those states, you have to meet some criteria to wholesale such as having a license as a real estate agent. it's safe to expect we will have more of those in the future.

For further learning

Pace Morby
   https://www.youtube.com/c/PaceMorby

Jerry Norton
   https://www.youtube.com/c/FlippingMasteryTV

6

Long Term Rental

This is probably the type of real estate investing you're most familiar with. You purchase a property and rent it out to a tenant or tenants, usually on a lease longer than one month (typically 12 months). This is called Long Term Rental (LTR) or just rental. Most likely, you have some experience being on the other end of this transaction as a tenant.

Pros

Relatively safe

People need a place to live in and not everyone can afford to buy a house, so the demand is almost always there, especially if you operate in a mid-price range neighborhood in a populous city. Since this is a long-tested investment strategy, there is plenty of technology, services, and people to support you (from tenant screening and collecting rents to property management at the site) if you choose to pursue this investment.

If a property is confirmed profitable as LTR, you can try some other strategy with more upside potential (e.g. Short Term Rental or coliving) while having LTR as a safety net.

Consistency and Predictability

Unlike Short Term Rental, which often suffers from seasonality, LTR provides more consistent income throughout the year.

Reaping benefits from ownership

Since you own a property, you enjoy all the benefits of the ownership mentioned earlier. Your property produces cash flow, might appreciate in value (depending on the market and the neighborhood you're in), and your tenant pays off your mortgage. Your day-to-day workload tends to be lower compared to wholesale once a tenant (especially a good one) is in place.

Ease of financing

A 30-year fixed rate is the most common financing product people use and financing is easier with consistency of Long Term Rental.

Cons

Relatively low return

Among various rental strategies, LTR tends to yield a lower return. When you go on a vacation, you might want to splurge on a hotel or luxury Airbnb, but it's usually not sustainable to pay those premiums for your residence on a regular basis. Also, LTR tenants receive less service compared to hotel or Airbnb guests (e.g. no housekeeping) and pay utilities themselves so it makes sense that LTR generates lower returns.

Hard to make it work in a tenant-friendly states

Some states are more favorable to landlords (typically red states: LA, AL, SC, NV, AR, WY, WV, IN) and other states are more favorable to tenants (typically blue states: CA, NY, OR, WA, MA, MN).

There is a term for those who abuse and take advantage of these tenant-friendly laws, Professional Tenant. They exploit legal loopholes and remain in a rental property without paying rent.

With that being said, there is a way for you to get into LTR even if you live in one of the tenant-friendly states. It is possible for you to own and rent a property in a state other than the state of your residence. With proper systems in place, it is definitely possible to do so although it is advisable for beginners to start in "your own backyard" (i.e. within driving distance from your residence).

Delayed Maintenance

Unlike Short Term Rental or Mid Term Rental, where cleaners will check the status of your property every few days to every few months, LTR landlords may not get to see the condition of the property for 12 months, 36 months, or even longer. This delayed and accumulated maintenance can result in substantial damage to the property, which could cost a lot to repair.

7

Short Term Rental (Vacation Rental)

Airbnb, founded in 2008, democratized Short Term Rental. There were other companies in this space such as Vrbo and Booking.com, but Airbnb truly made STR a household name. When you're on vacation, instead of staying at a hotel, some choose to stay at a place provided through one of those STR platforms, also known as Online Travel Agency (OTA).

Pros

Potentially higher return

When you are on vacation and stay at a hotel or an STR property for a couple of days, you might pay a higher price per day (average daily rate or ADR) compared to the amount of your "daily rent" (your monthly rent divided by 30). STR tends to provide more amenities and needs a higher rate of turnover (i.e. cleaning after guests check out), which drives up the cost of operation. So all these contribute to higher returns with STR compared to LTR.

That said, underwriting your deal is as crucial as any investment. I purchased a property and it has been losing money for months. I learned a ton from that deal but you shouldn't jump on a deal just to be able to say "I've done a deal." It doesn't feel great if your investment loses money month after month even just for a bit.

Tax benefits

Just like any other type of rental where you own a property, you get to enjoy tax benefits such as depreciation. If you get to do accelerated depreciation through cost segregation, you can reduce your tax bill significantly.

Ecosystem

There are a plethora of Property Management Systems or PMS (such as Hospitable, Guesty, Hostaway, Lodgify, OwnerRez, iGMS just to name a few) that help you manage your properties and bookings, automate tasks needed to serve your guests and work with your team (e.g. cleaners, handyperson). Smart Lock services such as RemoteLock along with compatible hardware would enable guests to check in without you being on site. Digital Guidebooks such as Touch Stay would help your guests get answers to their questions and reduce inquiries from your guests. Dynamic Pricing such as PriceLabs would help you maximize your revenue. Once you have all the necessary staff and systems in place, STR is manageable for many hosts even from a remote location.

Cons

High Involvement

With STR, your guests might ask you for things that LTR tenants won't, such as a lightbulb burning out. Also, STR guests won't be as familiar with your property as LTR tenants so you might have to handle more questions with STR.

Dependence on OTA

With STR, your business depends on OTA (such as Airbnb or Vrbo) to some degree until you solidify your direct booking flow. In case of dispute, they are somewhat inclined to favor guests (who bring revenue) rather than hosts.

Vulnerable to regulations

Many municipalities see STR as a cause of increasing housing prices and a threat to an inventory of affordable residences. As a result, there are ever-increasing regulations against STR across the country.

For further learning

Robuilt
https://www.youtube.com/c/Robuilt

The Real Estate Robinsons
https://www.youtube.com/c/therealestaterobinsons

Short Term Rental Long Term Wealth by Avery Carl
https://store.biggerpockets.com/products/short-term-rental-long-term-wealth

Boostly for direct booking
https://boostly.co.uk/

Google Vacation Rentals
https://support.google.com/hotelprices/answer/10062327?hl=en

8

Mid Term Rental

Mid Term Rental (MTR) is usually a stay longer than 1 month and shorter than 12 months. Arguably, you can say it's the best of both worlds between LTR and STR. MTR usually yields higher returns than LTR, but is immune to STR regulations. With Mid Term Rental, hosts usually sign a contract with institutions such as hospitals, insurance companies, and many other types of businesses. When a hospital has traveling nurses temporarily assigned, they use your MTR as a place for these staff to stay. Or when a family loses their home to a fire, their insurance company puts them in your MTR for a few months. Where there's a temporary housing need, MTR can provide value to these companies whether it's an oil company, a brewery, or a manufacturing facility.

Pros

Business to Business

Unlike LTR or STR, it can be more of a Business to Business (B2B) relationship and it tends to be a continuous business with less fluctuation especially if your MTR falls under the corporate housing category as opposed to remote workers.

Free from STR regulations

We are seeing ever-increasing STR regulations popping up across the nation. It's not uncommon for former STR operators to convert their properties to MTR.

Ecosystem

You can utilize many STR hardware and software services for MTR to automate your operation.

Cons

Higher cost of entry

Just like STR, you should furnish your property in addition to acquiring the property before putting it on MTR. Furnishing cost and more frequent turnover drives the operating expenditures of MTR/STR up compared to LTR.

Doesn't work everywhere

There has to be workforce demand in your market in order for MTR to work. There has to be a larger hospital, a factory, an airport, a fulfillment center, or some sort of business that requires temporary housing in the area. It's hard to make it work if you're in a very rural area.

For further learning

Jesse Vasquez
https://www.youtube.com/channel/UC2x-yFc6Dbtzul2eN_Iskgw

30-Day Stay (Book)
https://store.biggerpockets.com/products/30-day-stay

Furnished Finder
https://www.furnishedfinder.com/

ALE Solutions
https://www.alesolutions.com/

9

Tax Liens

When one owns a property, they owe property tax each year to the county where the property is in. If the homeowner is behind on the payment of the property tax, at one point, the county puts a lien called tax lien onto the property. This makes the homeowner unable to sell the property without paying the back tax to the county first.

Counties need this property tax income to pay and maintain teachers, firefighters, roads, and other infrastructure and services to the community. To compensate for the shortage of tax income, many counties sell these tax liens to investors. When these investors purchase a tax lien, they essentially loan money to the county on behalf of the homeowner at a predetermined interest rate (e.g. 18% in Florida).

Depending on the county, those tax liens are sold either at an in-person auction or on an online auction platform. If nobody bids on a tax lien at these auctions, it goes on sale over the counter, where investors can purchase these tax liens without going through an auction.

After you purchase a tax lien, you just basically wait until it "redeems" (i.e. the homeowner pays the back tax), at which point you get your principal back with interest. This is the "worst-case scenario" for the tax lien investor. If the homeowner doesn't pay the back tax they owe by the end of the redemption period, you (as a tax lien certificate holder) might become eligible to foreclose on the property. Then, the property goes to an auction and you can bid on the auction to win the property or if nobody bids, you might even receive the title to the property.

Pros

Relatively Passive

You obviously have to conduct your due diligence on a property before purchasing a tax lien, but once you purchase the tax lien, all you have to do is just wait. The most likely scenario is the homeowner decides to pay the back tax. Upon redemption, the county will cut you a check and you get your money back with interest. For the most part, you just wait doing nothing with the tax lien certificate.

Guaranteed by Government

With Tax Lien investing, your interaction is either with a county (i.e. a government entity) or the third-party auction platform (e.g. Real Auction) that the county has a contract with. This is a relatively low-risk investment.

Cons

Takes time and capital

There is a delay between your purchase of the tax lien and redemption. You have no control over that delay. It can take a few weeks or a couple of years. Unless you have a large enough portfolio of tax lien certificates, this strategy alone may not replace your W-2 income.

Required knowledge

Each county runs its tax sale differently. You need to know their rules. Also, it requires thorough research on the property.

10

Land

You can purchase a parcel of land (sometimes at a discount) and sell it to end buyers at a retail market price or to other land investors at a wholesale price. Sometimes, this is called land flipping. You can sell it as a one-time cash transaction (if a buyer plans to build a home relatively soon) or on terms (i.e. install payments over some time) using a legal document called Contract for Deed (CFD) or Land Contract depending on the state.

Why would one sell their parcel at a discount when you sell it and make profits? Sometimes, the current owner inherits from their late parents and the heirs have no use or interest (in some cases, these parcels are located hundreds of miles away from the place of their residence) yet they have to keep paying the property tax for it year after year. They would rather get rid of it even at a discount. Land investors provide a solution to their problems in these cases.

Pros

No Tenants, Toilets, or Termites

You are basically buying and selling dirt. There is no structure for buyers to live in (just yet at least), therefore, by definition, you cannot have typical issues that landlords have with their rental properties, usually called 3Ts (Tenants, Toilets, or Termites).

Relatively low acquisition cost

Compared to purchasing a house, a parcel of land costs significantly less (because there is no structure). This drives the upfront investment down, which makes it suitable for investors with relatively low investment capital at hand.

If you go for a parcel that is very rural, it can cost as little as $1,000. In those cases, it's not uncommon to close a deal (both on the acquisition side and disposition side) even without title companies or real estate agents because the fees you pay to these parties are too high relative to the profit you make in these transactions, it would stop making sense for investors to work with them. But if the parcel is worth more than $5,000 or 10,000, it would definitely be wise to work with them.

Cons

Sometimes hard to market and sell

Your product is dirt, which is sometimes hard to market compared to a house that you can live in. There's relatively little to show for it in your marketing material. There are no beautiful granite counters or stainless steel kitchen appliances that catch your buyer's eye. You need your buyers to have a vision about what they can do and build on the property or you need to help them to have that vision.

For Further Learning

Land Investing Online with Apke Brothers
  https://landinvestingonline.com/
  https://www.youtube.com/c/LandInvestingOnline

Land Profit Generator with Jack & Michelle Bosch
  https://www.landprofitgenerator.com/
  https://www.youtube.com/channel/UCtcHEhFMrVir6MXjqhRaeLQ

LandGeek
  https://www.thelandgeek.com/
  https://www.youtube.com/user/TheLandGeek

11

Lending

Technically, lending is not necessarily a real estate investment per se. It's a service provider to real estate investors (just like real estate agents are) but it's tightly connected to real estate investment and an integral part of real estate transactions, so I put it here as an honorable mention.

There are a few types of lending you can potentially step in as. If a real estate investor does fix-n-flip on a house, they get most of the money to purchase and renovate the house from an institution called a Hard Money Lender (HML), but usually, HML doesn't cover the whole cost to complete the project. A Private Money Lender (PML) can lend the remaining portion needed to finish the project.

HML is an entity/institution that lends money for business. PML is regular people (like your relatives), who might or might not have other jobs, and who happen to lend money as well. So you can be a PML without a license.

Also, you can be a transactional lender. Remember when we talked about wholesale? An increasing number of states have passed a law prohibiting real estate wholesale without the license of a real estate agent. Because of that, wholesalers in those states do more and more double close.

With double close, a wholesaler purchases a house from the seller and once that transaction with the seller (called A-B transaction) is closed, they immediately turn around and sell the property to the buyer (called B-C transaction). Note this is not a traditional wholesale transaction anymore. The wholesaler is not assigning a contract here. They become the owner of the property (with the title under their name) even for a brief moment before they sell it. In order for the A-B transaction to close, they need to give the full purchase price to the seller. Now, the wholesaler needs far more money upfront than they do in the case of a regular wholesale transaction. If you have enough funds to cover the A-B transaction, you can be a transactional lender. You can get your return on your investment within 24 hours with double close, whereas PML terms tend to be 6 to 12 months.

Pros

Relatively passive

Lending in general is relatively passive compared to rentals. You do have to do your due diligence, but once it's done, you wire money and follow up as the deal progresses and you wait for your money to be paid back to you with interest. You won't get a call on a plumbing issue on the weekend or in the middle of the night.

Quick turnaround time

Especially with double close, the time between you lending your money and you getting your money back is quite small. You can make a profit within 24 hours.

Cons

Requires due diligence on borrowers and/or their deals

When you lend your money either as a PML or transactional lender, you need to vet the borrower and/or the deals. For PML (for a fix-n-flip project), you need to vet the borrower and their expertise and experience on similar projects. For double close, you need to make sure that you and the title company/the closing attorney who handles escrow are on the same page.

Missing tax benefits

You, as a lender, don't own a property so you forgo tax benefits coming from ownership of properties.

12

Conclusion

There you have it! Over the last few years, I spent tens of thousands of dollars on courses and mentorships, read or listened to dozens of books/audible/podcasts, attended hundreds of zooms, made countless calls, and put my lessons learned down into this book. I really hope you've enjoyed this book as much as I've enjoyed writing it! And that it has helped you make your own decisions on your real estate investment journey a little bit.

If you found this book helpful, I'd be very appreciative if you left a favorable review for the book on Amazon. It would mean the world to me!

Again, thank you for taking this book and reading it. It's a cliché but time is the most valuable resource that one has. I'm grateful that you spent your time reading this book. As a fellow real estate investor, I'm rooting for you.

13

Resources

The benefits of owning real estate. (2022, March 1). Stone & Browning Property Management. Retrieved April 7, 2024, from https://stonebrowningpm.com/the-benefits-of-owning-real-estate

Voigt, K. (2024, March 22). Best-Performing REITs: How to invest in real estate investment trusts. NerdWallet. Retrieved April 7, 2024, from https://www.nerdwallet.com/article/investing/reit-investing

Luthi, B. (2023, September 7). Pros and Cons of investing in REITs. Experian. Retrieved April 7, 2024, from https://www.experian.com/blogs/ask-experian/pros-cons-investing-in-reits/

NT Capital, LLC. (2023, September 28). 8 Top Pros & Cons of Syndication Investing. Passive Wealth Strategy Show - Passive Wealth with Real Estate. Retrieved April 7, 2024, from https://www.passivewealthstrategy.com/8-pros-cons-syndication-investing/

Blumenfeld, A. (2024, March 22). GP vs LP: A Comparison Guide For Real Estate Investors. EquityMultiple. Retrieved April 7, 2024, from https://equitymultiple.com/blog/gp-vs-lp

Marten, G. (2023, February 28). 7 Pros & 3 Cons Of Wholesaling Real Estate. How to Invest in Real Estate. Retrieved April 7, 2024, from https://leadflow.com/blog/pros-cons-of-wholesaling-real-estate

Advantages and Disadvantages of Long-Term Rentals. (2021, April 13). Landmark Property Management. Retrieved April 7, 2024, from https://www.chicagospropertymanagement.com/blog/advantages-and-disadvantages-of-long-term-rentals

Welty, S. (2024, February 22). Short-term rental vs. long-term rental: 12 Things to Know. Good Life Property Management. Retrieved April 7, 2024, from https://www.goodlifemgmt.com/blog/short-term-rental-vs-long-term-rental/

McCann, K. (2024, March 6). Mid-Term rentals: Pros and cons for property owners - Azibo. azibo.com. Retrieved April 7, 2024, from https://www.azibo.com/blog/mid-term-rentals-pros-and-cons-for-property-owners

Foster, S. (2024, February 28). Tax lien investing: What to know before jumping in. Bankrate Press. Retrieved April 7, 2024, from https://www.bankrate.com/investing/investing-in-tax-liens-fraught-with-risk/

LandyDandy. (2023, October 12). Is land flipping worth it? Factors to consider before investing | Vacant Land Expert Blog | LandyDandy. Retrieved April 7, 2024, from https://landydandy.com/is-land-flipping-worth-it/

www.ingramcontent.com/pod-product-compliance
Lightning Source LLC
Chambersburg PA
CBHW070955220526
45471CB00007B/3043